Picture Perfect Presentations

The Complete Guide to Creating Dynamic Presentations for Every Situation

Written by

Elliott Eddie

ISBN: **0692227563**
ISBN-13: **978-0-692-22756-5**

CONTENTS

The Art of Storytelling:

Painting a Perfect Picture with Words.

The purpose of this guide is a bit different from the norm. A lot of times we look at great orators and we attempt to model ourselves after them. For example, when you watch a movie or TV show, almost everyone who plays a preacher uses a "Martin Luther King Junior" voice. You know the voice.

The point is - becoming a dynamic presenter is not about changing who you are, or modeling your speaking style after someone else. Being a dynamic presenter is about continuing to improve your own technique. Being a better presenter is about taking your personal speaking style and your personality and playing to your strengths.

For example, one of my strengths in my presentations is my ability to create realistic and believable characters. So in most of my presentations I will often incorporate a story that will allow me to bring at least one major character life. Perhaps it will be a 103-year old man with arthritis, a bad hip and a mind as sharp as a tack. Perhaps I will bring to life an eccentric jeweler with a flair for scarves and turrets syndrome, who makes jewels for the queen of England. I have even brought to life a five-year old girl playing with her teddy bear, full of sound advice and dying from cancer. My goal is to bring real people to life so that listeners can experience a moment in time through their eyes, laugh and cry with these characters, and ultimately in the end, learn a lesson that will improve their lives in some way.

This book is a complete guide on how to create the most dynamic presentations possible. To accomplish this goal, we will focus on two sides of creating a dynamic presentation:

1. **Speech Crafting**

2. **Storytelling**

SPEECH CRAFTING

The speech crafting portion is important to every presentation you will give- no matter the type. This portion of the book will give you not only the basics of speech crafting, but also advanced techniques to engage more of your audiences' senses to get them fully involved in your presentation from the first sentence.

STORYTELLING

Storytelling is extremely important to the success of your presentation. The storytelling portion of this book will help you understand why stories are important in your presentation and how to create and incorporate incredible stories to use to explain your points or your message.

To create a great story, we must keep in mind the main thing our audience is longing for. Your listeners want to experience the story with you and with the characters. Audiences want to go on the adventure with you as their guide. Your audience wants to discover the plot with you because they want to identify the people they relate to.

The way a speaker structures his or her story will allow the listeners to participate- to become emotionally connected to the characters and the story. Then you, as the storyteller, will guide them to the finish, which will always be your main message.

What are the elements of an effective story? Before I answer that, let's consider this question, what is an effective story? For the sake of clarity, let's define what an effective story is. This way, we can all be on the same page.

An effective story, as defined for this guide is,

"A story that takes your listeners on a journey, allowing everyone to arrive at the point of your message at the same time".

To help accomplish this, we will go over a number of steps that will help you take your presentations to the next level. Following these steps will allow you to create presentations and training sessions that will keep your audience's attention throughout the entire presentation.

If by chance you are an actor or other type of performance artist, these steps will help you blow your audiences away with intense and dramatic presentations. We accomplish this by first laying down some basic ground work that will help create a picture perfect presentation. Then we will go deeper into the mechanics of creating awesome stories that can be inserted into the presentations.

Most people speakers and audiences don't know this information. Audiences and speakers will be amazed at how different your presentations are than all the others they are listening to. Following this guide will give you the most unique and engaging presentations anyone has ever seen.

You are going to be awesome!

1 HOW TO IDENTIFY YOUR PRESENTATION'S PURPOSE

Speaking in front of people, large crowds in particular is usually perceived as the most stressful experience imaginable. The following ideas in this guide are designed to help you, or *anyone* for that matter, convey your ideas and messages to either one person, or a large group in just about *any* setting. Creating an effective presentation, can seem very overwhelming. But here are strategies you can use to come up with an effective and powerful speech in 30 minutes or less, regardless of your target audience.

#1 Identifying your purpose

- Begin with the end in mind

- The essence of public speaking is not to GAIN but to GIVE

- What is the 'call to action' for your speech?

How to Identify your purpose

The importance of goal-setting must not be overlooked when preparing for any presentation. The very first thing you need do before you even embark on your presentation is to define your objectives. It is crucial that you **begin with the end in mind**. Ask yourself this, "What do I want to achieve from my speech?", "What do I want my audience to receive?", and "What do I want my audience to do next?"

The first thing to do in the speech preparation process is to **identify your purpose**. The purpose of your presentation can range from creating awareness, fostering understanding, generating impact, selling a product, inspire your audience or just entertain. Remember that the main reason why you're presenting in the first place is to **give, not just gain**. As such, your goals should be aligned with allowing your audience to benefit from your presentation. Your purpose-setting must be extremely clear, not just to yourself, but to your audience as well. This helps them internally craft the benefits they will gain from listening to you.

One of the biggest mistakes of public speaking is when you start with the wrong purpose in mind. A number of speakers operate without a specific purpose which can easily cause stress and anxiety. The nature of your purpose is *just as important* as the purpose itself. Many speakers often mistakenly assume or even subconsciously decide that their purpose is audience validation and approval. Not True. Setting audience validation as a purpose causes great pressure on the speaker to be absolutely perfect in order to win unanimous approval and this causes a great deal of anxiety. I call this a "stress-producing" purpose.

Once you've established the purpose of your presentation, you can easily craft your presentation around it in order for it to be achieved. Remember that the essence of public speaking is not to GAIN something, but to GIVE something. When you operate with that frame of mind, you automatically tune your body language, tone of voice and craft content that is useful for your audience. With that, you immediately attract the attention of the majority.

To conclude this section, here's a quick summary. <u>Before even writing your speech, you need to clearly define your objectives and ask yourself, "What do you want to achieve with this?"</u> and to set goals that benefit not just yourself, but your audience as well. Now that you've identified the purpose of your speech, you can move on to the next stage.

#2 Preparing your speech

- Does the speech pass the 'business card' test?

- Draft your speech with 4-5 key points

#2 How To Prepare A Speech

Now that you've identified the *purpose* of your speech, it's time you craft it. But before you do, it's important to **clarify your topic.** One way to make sure you've got it all cleared up is to try out the "business card test" - can you state your main idea on only *one* side of a business card? If you can, you're ready to move on. If you can't, keep working on it until you can.

Now you can start drafting your speech. Grab a sheet of paper and right at the top of the page, clearly state your desired topic and the goal of your presentation. Then move on to write your opening lines and follow that up with 4-5 key points. Back these points up and summarize them in the conclusion. This is your outline. Now that you've listed your most important subjects, you can begin crafting your presentation based on the completed outline.

Before you start writing your speech out proper, let's take a quick detour and visit one of the greatest and most notable speeches made in human history - yes, Martin Luther King, Jr.'s "I Have A Dream". Did you know that the most important, most often-quoted and the most powerful part of his entire speech, his iconic "I have a dream" statement, was made only in the last quarter of his entire powerful presentation? It makes you wonder how he managed to capture the full attention of over 200,000 agitated, and angry civil rights supporters? If you were thinking that it was his authority, you're wrong. And it wasn't his looks either. Reverend King had a powerful introduction. He started with this,

"Five score years ago, a great American, in whose symbolic shadow we stand today, signed the Emancipation Proclamation. This momentous decree came as a great beacon light of hope to millions of Negro slaves who had been seared in the flames of withering injustice. It came as a joyous daybreak to end the long night of their captivity."

Martin Luther King, Jr. started his powerful speech with a strong, passionate story which set the mood for the rest of his speech. When you begin crafting your speech, you have to remember that the most important part is **your introduction**. If your audience's attention is not captured within the first 30 seconds, you're pretty much history. Your introduction can make, or break, your entire speech. Remember that a strong opening is King, pun unintended. You may start with a probing question, a strong statement, a personal story or even a quote. These elements not only set the mood for your speech, but also pique your audience's attention and focus sufficiently to hook them for the rest of what you have to say.

The idea of starting with a story is not a new idea, but it is an immensely effective one. Stories have the ability to engage a listener's imagination instantly and wisk them away into the world of your story. Starting with a story is powerful.

There are different ways to incorporate a story into the beginning of the speech. You can begin at the beginning of the story and follow it through. You can begin in the middle of the story or at one of it's "action points" and engage the audience in the drama from the start. You can then make your points and complete the story by going back and telling the audience what happened before the moments of drama and how the situation played out. Of course the situation will play out the perfect way it needs to help solidify the point or message of your speech. Still there are times when you may want to start at the end of the speech and then take us back to the beginning.

However you decide to start the story, make sure you let the audience know in the first minute of your story the "who, where, when and what the conflict is".

Now that you've crafted a powerful introduction, you can move on to the core points of your speech. Each of these points should be backed by interesting stories, illustrations, historical references, humorous anecdotes, and examples that the audience is able to relate to. Common stories or illustrations include references to common childhood occurrences, "growing up" pains or even teenage experiences. You can use these stories and examples to further reinforce your point. Humans are sensory creatures. If you're able to pique more than just one sense - their hearing - you've got them hooked, forever. Remember to include descriptives in your stories and even images for the visual ones in your audience. Analogies help your audience connect the dots of your points in their heads. Also remember to open and close each point with a clear transition. This makes it easier for your audience to follow your story.

For those of you who are selling to or motivating your audience, you may even address your audience's pain. Stress the benefits of taking immediate action. Suggest a recommended course of action followed by closing remarks.

Now that you've detailed all the main points of your speech, you can start to **write your close**. A common, but effective, conclusion is a summary. This can be followed by an appeal or a call to action to challenge your audience, which is completely dependent on your purpose and topic. Run a quick summary by your audience and if necessary, outline clear guidelines and next actions they can take with the information you've just given them so that they do not feel like they've left your speech with nothing concrete to take with them.

#2 Preparing your speech

- Identify your purpose
- Clarify your topic
- Draft your speech
- Craft your introduction
- List the main points you wish to convey
- Write your close and end your speech

Here's a quick summary of the preparation process:

1. Identify your purpose
2. Clarify your topic
3. Draft your speech
4. Craft your introduction
5. List the main points you wish to convey
6. Write your close and end your speech with clear step-by-step or listed guides or next actions for your audience.

Let's move on to the next part of this guide.

#3 Preparing your visual aids

- Flip charts
- Font
- Colors
- K.I.S.S.
- Less is more

#3 How to incorporate visual aids

In Martin Luther King, Jr.'s time, visual aids weren't just a luxury - they were a hassle, and in some cases, an impossibility. Thanks to technological advances today, you have projectors in almost every main hall of a speaking event, or a *white board* with markers at the very least. As such, it's no excuse to *not* have visual aids accompanying your speech.

Why are visual aids so important? They stimulate another one of your audience's senses and force their brain to link the two together. This inadvertently helps keep them awake and focused throughout your speech. Most importantly, they allow you to further reinforce your points to your audience, and increase the number of associations their brain makes- which can heighten your audience's recall of your topic. Let me share with you two very commonly used, and highly effective, visual aids that will captivate your audience's attention and help cue you as your speak.

Firstly, **flip charts**. Flip charts are huge pads of paper that are mounted on a portable easel. This visual aid is best used with a relatively small audience - typically 20 or fewer - unless there's a camera to magnify the chart for the rest of the hall. You can use bold or dark colors against a white flip chart to increase the ease of reading. A flip chart can be prepared *prior* to your presentation, but the power of the flip chart is that it can be used for drawing or writing *during* your presentation. Many motivational speakers adopt the flip chart, why? Because in comparison with PowerPoint presentations, a flip chart allows the presenter to have a wider range of body movement in order to reinforce and reiterate their points with gestures and force.

Next up, you've got the PowerPoint presentation. These days using a laptop, a projector and Microsoft PowerPoint or the Apple Keynote program is the norm. Technological advances have allowed us to produce dramatic, high-resolution visual aids such as animation and simulations. Today, computer-based visual aids are becoming the standard for many technical, educational and even business-related presentations. The power of the PowerPoint presentation is that it can be used for both small and large audiences and can convey both simple and highly complex information. Today, with remote control devices, you can even change your visuals as you walk about the stage. If you've ever watched TED videos online, or attended a TED Talk, you'll know what I mean. The challenge with computer-based visuals is that you need to keep them simple. There are *many* things to consider when crafting your presentation. Here are a few you can keep in mind.

Firstly, your **font**. Not only is font-size important, your *choice* of font affects readability significantly. Always stick to high readability fonts such as "Times New Roman", "Arial" or "Helvetica". San-serif fonts are preferred as they usually increase readability. If these fonts seem "boring" or "distasteful" to you, scrap that thought. Your audience will thank you profusely for using these fonts.

Secondly, your **colors**. Choose colors that heighten readability. Remember that red text against a black background is a terror to read, and the same for vice-versa. Stick to pale, pastel backgrounds and dark text color such as black, or dark, black/brown backgrounds and white text color. And remember that your text should only have a maximum of **three** colors. If you fear that your presentation has become monotone, you can always opt for colorful images and pictures to add a splash of life to your slideshow. But remember to choose your pictures wisely and to not let them upstage you and your speech.

Thirdly, **K.I.S.S**. Yes, keep it simple and suggestive. I'm talking about the text. It's a presentation faux pas to *read your slides* to your audience. You should know everything inside out and only occasionally turn to your slides for a cue or reference. Most importantly, the main points of your presentation should *not* be in your visual aids. The text in your visual aids should only allude to your main points. Use bullet points instead of full sentences in order to decrease the wordiness of your visual aid. This also applies for your charts and diagrams. Don't present them a full-fledged chart with 20 components to decipher. If your presentation requires charts and graphs, slice the data for your audience beforehand. They don't need to know *everything* - only your key findings and the significant statistics.

Lastly, **less is more**. This is in reference to your animation. You can use animation to reiterate a point, or even create some drama and suspense. But to animate *every single word* or object in your presentation is a *huge* no-no. Not only will you heavily distract your audience, you may also give them a headache.

To quickly summarize, flip charts are great to use with smaller crowds and give you wider range of movement. If you're considering using PowerPoint or keynote slides as a visual aid, remember the 4 rules to increase readability and audience attention:

1. Simple font
2. High contrast and minimal colors
3. Keep it simple and suggestive
4. Less animation is more.

Visual aids are huge help for presentations and should be used if possible. However, avoid the number one mistake made by many novice speakers: Do not let your visual aids control you. You control the presentation. Your visual aid is merely an "aid" and is not the entire show. Use it to reiterate and back up your points and don't make it the point of the *entire* presentation. Remember that the point of your visual aid is to motivate your audience and arouse their imagination to help them to empathize with your idea and topic and visualize it far beyond what is visible in the ephemeral PowerPoint slide they currently view.

Now that you've got speech and presentation basics covered, let's move on to something a little bit more practiced.

#4 Creating a mock presentation

- Smile and speak aloud

- Record your rehearsal

- **Pay attention to body language!**

#4 How to eliminate stress and fear

Creating a mock presentation

The one way to eliminate stress and fear **before** your presentation day is to **rehearse**. Consistent practice will not only *significantly* boost your confidence, but it will also help you **remember and become more accustomed to your material**. Let me run through with you the basic structure of a rehearsal.

First, memorize your opening sentence. This is crucial as once you've got into the beat of things; you'll realize that the rest flows in more smoothly. Next, memorize your main points in order of your presentations. Try to come up with acronyms for your points and run them in your head consistently while preparing. This will help greatly with you memorization of the material and the order of the material. Also, remember your transitions. In between each point, remember your choice of transition into the next point. Relate your transition sentence to your main point and you will easily recall it during your actual presentation. Lastly, remember your stories. The best way to do so is not to create stories, but to use actual personal experiences. This way you won't have to try too hard to memorize details and feelings, but the story itself will come naturally to you and even if you forget the flow of the story, you'll have your memory to help you. Once you have become better at your presentations, you can begin to become a little more creative with your storytelling. We will talk more about storytelling creation techniques later in the book.

While practicing, it's important to **smile and speak aloud**, even if you're alone. Believe me when I say that presenting in your head is not the same as speaking it aloud. Simulating an actual presentation even when alone can help you build confidence and help you create the atmosphere of an actual presentation. When I say simulate - I mean go all out. Smile, use gestures, refer to your visual aids, practice your posture - all this may seem silly, but it really helps increase your energy and enthusiasm, indirectly injecting this same energy into your audience on the real day.

When you simulate your presentation to an actual audience, start by getting your friends and family to help you out. If you get nervous when speaking to a large audience. Start small. Start out practicing to an audience of 2 - your parents or siblings perhaps. Gather their feedback and move on to a larger practice group of 4. Ask your friends for a hand and get them to sit in and provide you with their honest opinions. Then move on a practice group of 8, and repeat this process to a larger group of friends. Remember to obtain feedback from every group and reflect on your flaws and the specific things that you can improve on. Remember to ask your audience to be critical and nitpick on all your presentation flaws. You want to be able to learn from your mistakes, big or small, before the real thing. One great thing you can do is join a local Toastmasters club. Toastmasters International is a worldwide organization and there are clubs meeting in a City and Town near you.

Another important thing to do is to **record your rehearsal**. Record it in video format if you can. Why do I suggest recording? This is so you can reflect on your own presentation aside from your audience. Put yourself in the shoes of a viewer or listener and identify your mistakes or less glorious moments. Focus your attention on the pacing and timing of your speech as well and take notes for your following practice. You can easily record your speech with a cell phone for now. If you do your speech in front of friends or family members, ask one of them to tape the presentation for you.

Lastly, your **body language** is particularly important as they send subliminal messages to your audience. Walk straight and tall, make constant and firm eye contact with your audience, smile consistently and use gestures to help inject some versatility and movement into your presentation. Not only will this convey a less wooden message to your audience, this can also help to dissipate nervous tension. Relax as much as you can and have fun.

To quickly summarize - **practice, reflect, practice.** That's the key to presentation success. Rehearse to small groups, slowly increase the headcount in those groups and obtain feedback from your mock audience. Record your rehearsals and analyze your own speech and presentation style and place particular emphasis on your body language.

5 HOW TO ELIMINATE STAGE FRIGHT AND BUILD SELF-CONFIDENCE

#1 Eliminate stage fright and build your self confidence

- Fear is **not** pain, but the mere **anticipation** of it

- 5 causal elements of stage fright: imagination of people judge, possibility of failure, inherent need to do well, feeling of uncertainty, excessive focus on one's own behavior and appearance

Eliminate stage fright and build your self-confidence

Are you the type who cringes at the *thought* of walking on stage? The type that is overcome by sweaty palms, a racing heartbeat and shaky legs the moment you take your first step on that platform. If you are, don't think of yourself any less. Fear of public speaking is highly common and almost everyone has experienced or felt it at one point in their lives. Statistics show that some degree of public speaking fear affects an estimated **95%** of all speakers. In fact, recent studies in the United States of America have shown that fear of public speaking actually ranks higher than fear of death! Don't you find it bizarre that the general American public fear facing crowds more than the prospect of Heaven or Hell?

That being said - let's dissect this common feeling in order to understand it better. Let's start with "what is fear"? Fear is defined as:

The **anticipation of pain**.

Yes, you heard that right. Fear is **not** pain, but the mere **anticipation** of it. There are 5 causal elements of stage fright:

1. The perception or imagination of the presence of people who will judge,

2. The possibility of failure,

3. The inherent need to do well in order to avoid failure,

4. The feeling of uncertainty of whether one can do well

5. An excessive focus on one's own behavior and appearance.

The reason why we experience uncomfortable symptoms like light-headedness, sweaty palms, and increased heart rate is because this fear is actually a psychological condition that is manifested physically via these symptoms! So in order to prevent these symptoms, we have to **conquer fear**. How do we do this? By attacking every one of the 5 causal symptoms. In this chapter I'll reveal **6 very simple steps to** help you **overcome your fear** of speaking to audiences on stage.

#1 Eliminate stage fright and build your self confidence

- **Step 1: Be audience-centered**
- **Step 2: Accept that you make mistakes**
- **Step 3: Ditch all that negative self-talk**
- **Step 4: Convert your fear into positive energy**
- **Step 5: Present daily**
- **Step 6: Practice Makes Near Perfect**

Step 1: Be audience-centered.

In order to conquer fear, you have to remember that your presentation is **not about yourself.** Instead, it's really about your audience. Focus on the needs of your audience, rather than on how you will perform and your fears will disappear. The truth is that no one really cares about your voice, or how you look. Your audience is more interested in what you have to offer them. Concentrate on how you can provide optimum benefit to the people listening to you. If you're selling a product, concentrate your efforts on selling the benefits of your product to your audience. If you're sharing learning, focus on how they can benefit or take action with what you have to share. Whether or not you are telling a story to build rapport, or delivering a sales pitch, a focus on your audience's needs can help take your mind off your fear.

Step 2: Accept that you make mistakes

No one is born a perfect speaker. Good public speakers aren't born, they're made. Do you think Martin Luther King, Jr. delivered that amazing speech on his first try? That man was a Reverend who had delivered countless speeches and sermons prior to "I Have A Dream". Even he made mistakes. So if you mess up, does it *really* matter? What's most important is that you **learn from your mistakes**. If you notice a mistake during your speech, no one in the audience is going to disapprove if you backtrack to amend that mistake. In fact, it's more credible that you do. In order to improve and **be** better, you have to take risks. Think of your presentation as an opportunity to benefit and convey amazing information to your audience. And remember this; Thomas Edison failed thousands of times before he invented the light bulb. And did it deter him? No. His inventions are spread across the world today and are constantly innovated upon. Do you want to be a Thomas Edison, or the person who's too afraid to leave his house for fear he falls?

Step 3: Ditch all that negative self-talk

If you remember the causal elements of stage fright I just mentioned, you'll notice that all of those elements have a recurring theme - negative self-talk. Just like how the seeds of a tree determine its fruits or end product, what happens on the inside has a significant impact on our outside. This means that our actions and fears are actually influenced by our subconscious minds. Negative self-talk not only drains your energy, it de-motivates you. In order to overcome this, you need to start replacing negative self-talk with positive talk. Stand in front of the mirror daily, straight-backed and with a smile on your face. Replace your "I can't do this", "People will judge me" and "I'm going to be terrible" thoughts with phrases like "I feel energetic!", "I'm prepared and focused!", "I am delivering value to my audience!" and "The audience is my friend, not foe." Eventually, the attitude and actions will follow. Just as Henry Ford once said,

"Whether you think you can or you think you can't, you're right".

Step 4: Convert your fear into positive energy.

Did you know that aside from your thoughts, you can also convert your physical behavior? You can help convert stage fright symptoms with the power of visualization and belief. For example, did you know that sweaty palms and a racing pulse are also symptoms of an adrenaline rush? So instead of attributing negative thoughts to your racing pulse and sweaty palms, why don't you decipher these physical reactions as an adrenaline rush? As excitement and optimism for your presentation? This not only decreases your fear, it also immediately turns on the alertness and energy switch in your body. Your physical reactions are what you make them to be.

Aside from that, if you find yourself blanking out midway through your presentation, don't panic. You can choose one of two routes. You can either; be honest, tell your audience you forgot and need to refer to your notes and laugh it off with a joke on aging, or you can side track a little and tell your audience a story of a funny thing that happened to you recently. Both routes give you a minute to realign your thoughts, give the audience a minute to laugh and humanize you to your audience.

If dry throat is your stage fright symptom, tell the organizers beforehand to prepare a glass of warm water or tea (cold drinks constrict your throat and cause more discomfort than comfort) and take an occasional sip in between your points. This not only gives your audience a minute to take notes, you are also offered a moment to recoup your thoughts and ready yourself for your next section. Remember to only take a sip though, and not gulp the entire glass down.

Step 5: Present daily

I'm not just talking about practice (I'll get into that later); I'm talking about incorporating it into your daily life. To tell you the truth, speaking to an audience is no different from your day-to-day interaction with the people around you. In a conversation, you're either trying to convey a message or sell an idea - both require the same skills and elements in a public presentation. Once you grasp and understand this concept, this can help you feel much more confident and powerful on stage. When you're talking to your friends, try to visualize yourself on a stage and imagine that they are your audience - how they react to you in that scenario is really how they will react to you on stage, with the exception that your friends can actually interrupt you. One way of gaining confidence and overcoming fear, is to incorporate elements of your public speaking skills into your daily conversations with your boss, colleagues, friends and family. Take careful notice of how they respond and you can easily tweak your conversation style to produce your desired reactions.

Step 6: Practice Makes Near Perfect.

I'm repeating this point from our last session because it is **that important**. This may seem simple enough, but the more you know your material, the more confident you'll be. The fear of forgetting will disappear almost entirely. Like I mentioned previously, practice your speech on 2 people, then 4, 8 and so on. Carefully assess your feelings whether it's confidence or anxiety throughout the presentation and record your practice groups' feedback. Remember that it doesn't have to be perfect. It will get better as you go along and practice more. With time and sufficient practice, your presentation skills will drastically improve to the extent that you no longer have to worry about embarrassing yourself or messing up.

Before we move on to the next point, let me quickly summarize the 6 steps to help overcome stage fright:

1. Be audience-centered
2. Accept that you can make mistakes
3. Ditch your negative self-talk
4. Convert your fear into positive energy
5. Present daily
6. Practice makes near perfect.

Now that you've got the basics of presentation preparation and the steps to eliminate stage fright, let's move on to **personalizing your presentation**.

6 HOW TO INCORPORATE YOUR PERSONALITY INTO YOUR PRESENTATION

#2 Incorporating your personality into your presentation

- Integrate personal stories

- Illustrate your physical style

- Keep your jewelry to a minimum

- Humor injects personality into your speech

Incorporating your personality into your presentation

One common trait among great presenters is that they have a distinct style which makes your speech memorable and helps inject *your* personality into your presentation. This helps keep your audience excited. President Obama often incorporates slogans and refrains in his speeches, and Steve Jobs was a visual-zen master who designs strategic placements of **empty** slides in order to make his images stronger

31

and more prominent when they appear. Like President Obama and Steve Jobs, you need to allocate time to focus on conveying your style in the most exciting manner possible.

One way to incorporate your personality is to **integrate personal stories** in your speech. This is not only an effective way of exposing your audience to who you are, it also helps them relate with you at a more emotional and personal level. One kind of personal story that usually does the trick is the success / hero story. You can speak of yourself as someone who overcame a huge obstacle in life that is relevant to your topic of presentation. This not only allows the audience to relate, sympathize and empathize with you, but also adds some credibility and authority to what you are about to share with them.

Another way of embodying your personality in your presentation is to **illustrate your physical style**. In other words, by how you dress. It's important to look the part of the message you're trying to convey. Top Internet marketer, Frank Kern's, selling point is **freedom**. This is why whenever he speaks to audiences, he's in surf shorts, a loose t-shirt with his hair in wild disarray - he's subliminally conveying the message of **freedom** to his audience. That being said, there are a few guidelines you should take into account when deciding what to wear on stage.

Firstly, keep your jewelry to a minimum. Adorning yourself with too much "bling" can distract your audience from your speech and the only thing they'll take back with them at the end of your presentation will be how bright and shiny you were. Secondly, stay away from overly colorful articles of clothing. A pair of pants with stripes in 5 contrasting colors will only remind them of a clown from their childhood, and not a person of authority. That being said, overly monotonous clothing may help blend you into the background, making you irrelevant and completely unmemorable to your audience. Your clothing should only *reiterate* your point, not run the show. Always remember that the audience's main focus should be on what you have to share with them, and nothing else.

Humor is another great way to inject some personality into your presentation. Not only can it help grasp your audience's attention, it can also liven up the atmosphere. However, if you choose to use humor in the presentation, make sure your jokes are original, and not cliché. Try not to make fun of members of your audience and instead turn the joke on yourself. For example, if you are a person of short stature, you may want to poke fun at your height to illustrate a point that is relevant to your speech. If you notice that your jokes are falling flat on the audience, don't be dejected. Punctuate them with short, nonchalant quips such as "I'll remember to keep that to myself the next time." or even "Well, my mom thought it was funny. I'll remember not to ask for her advice on humor next time".

At the end of the day, incorporating personality basically means **be yourself**. Your audience may not be psychic, but they will be able to see through a false persona. Therefore there is no better physical presentation than your **genuine self**. So relax, loosen up, and remind yourself to have a great time. A relaxed presenter who's enjoying his or herself automatically opens up the audience and loosens them up. Your audience is a mirror of who you project yourself to be.

#3 Extra stuff you need to help you convey a high-impact message

- Platform skills

- Allow a wide range of pitches and tones

- Your body language and gestures

- Invoke **attention, interest and emotion**

Extra stuff you need to help you convey a high-impact message

Let me share with you some extra elements you can add to give your presentation that extra "zing" it needs to go from good to great.

Platform skills play a pretty crucial role in getting your audience to not just pay attention to you but to also get them excited and enthusiastic about your message. The pacing of your presentation, the pitch, tone and volume of your voice and even your vocal variety play important roles in helping you convey your message effectively. These tools help you clarify and support your message, emphasize your ideas, and even dramatize your message. Consistently maintaining a high volume and loud tone of voice will make you come across as excessively authoritative or aggressive, while using low volumes and soft tones may make you come across as too timid and decrease your credibility as a speaker and the lack of variation will make you sound too monotonous.

The best and most effective route is to allow yourself a wide range of pitches and tones. Adding variety to your vocal pattern is a surefire way to engage your audience's attention and reinforce key ideas to them. In addition to that, a well-timed moment of silence or pause can help you further emphasize certain ideas, or in some situations, dramatize your message with a little suspense or anticipation. Some good uses of pauses include pausing after you tell a joke to provide emphasis, and give your audience a moment to quiet their laughter. Another good use of the pause is right after you're introduced to your audience as it gives them time to refocus their attention on the presentation.

Aside from your tone of voice, your body language and gestures are also important components in relaying a more meaningful and memorable speech by adding punctuation. Did you know that the human body contains more than 700 muscles? It's sad to know that only a handful of those muscles are used by speakers. Speakers tend to focus most of their attention in the search of the perfect words and the most precious points, thereby forgetting that our bodies speak louder than words ever could. When I say body language, I don't mean using your arms and fingers in a death grip clutch on a poor lectern, or frenetically clicking on your PowerPoint slides - I mean allowing your body to move naturally.

While a good message is important in a presentation, your effectiveness as speaker is really about your ability to invoke attention, interest and emotion in your audience through non-verbal communication. An amazing message conveyed with terrible body language does *not* get the point across. Why is that? Because your listeners don't only judge you and your message based on what they hear - they also take in to consideration what they *see*.

When speaking to an audience, your body can be used as a very effective tool for adding emphasis and clarity to your words. It also plays a very important role in convincing your audience of your sincere feelings, your earnestness in educating or sharing with them, and your enthusiasm about your topic. No matter the purpose of your speech, the exterior self that you project must be appropriate and relevant to what you say.

How to incorporate good body language

- Maintaining eye contact with your audience (3-5 seconds)

- 'Plant' a listener to watch out for distracting mannerisms

- Allow your body to move naturally

- Lastly, remember to smile!

Here are a few ways you can incorporate good body language into your presentations. Firstly, you can start with maintaining eye contact with your audience. You should not just continuously pass your gaze throughout the room; instead, try focusing your sight on individual members of the audience. You'll find that you can create a bond with them *just* by looking them directly in the eyes for 3-5 seconds. By using eye contact, you make everyone in your audience feel involved and connected to you.

Secondly, while in a practice session have a listener watch out for distracting mannerisms such as fidgeting, twitching, lip-biting, or key jingling. All these traits distract your audience from the key point of the message and focus their attention on your nervousness and fear. You then immediately discredit yourself of any authority that you have on what you're talking about. You automatically seem unsure, and decrease the amount of trust your audience has about your message.

Thirdly, allow your body to move naturally by moving from one spot of the stage or platform to another. A good example is to walk to the other side of the stage as you move on to your next point, or move toward the audience when you ask a question. These subtle moves help your audience to subconsciously visualize your transition from a point to another and help emphasize certain topics.

Lastly, remember to smile and actually express your emotions with your face. A smile can go a long way in helping the audience open up to you. That being said, constantly smiling throughout the entire speech only makes you look clinically insane. A variety of facial expressions that are relevant to what you're speaking about at the time can help you further punctuate your message. Surprise, curiosity, sadness, anger - these are but a handful of emotions that you can use while telling your audience a story in order for them to properly visualize it.

In summary, platform skills and effective use of body language can help you further punctuate your message and deliver a killer presentation. The keys to using them wisely? Variety and relevance. Always vary your tone of voice and body movements and always use them with relevance to whatever you're saying at the time.

Now that we've covered crafting your presentation, personalizing it and making it extraordinary, we can move on to more advanced stuff. In this session, we'll talk about ways to help you deal with an audience you've never met before and how to connect with them. In addition to that, we'll also cover the important and often nerve-wrecking Q&A session that normally follows a presentation.

8 HOW TO CREATE MAXIMUM IMPACT WITH YOUR AUDIENCE

#1 Surveying the audience

- Speak to them personally before speech

- Look around to decipher the general age-group

- Ascertain if your cultural references are relevant

- Quickly assess their careers and stages of life.

Surveying the audience

Another core component of a killer presentation is audience interaction. The final part of any presentation - answering questions from the audience - can help you build trust and further establish your credibility as an expert on your subject. Just keep in mind that this part of the presentation is the one part where you have close to no control over. Therefore the first step to succeeding in this arena is to **getting to know your audience better**.

Prior to your presentation, you should do a quick survey of your audience. There are a few ways you can do this and these methods are completely dependent on the nature of your presentation. If you're one of several speakers presenting to a large crowd of people, you may want to take a few minutes to mingle with your audience *before* your speech. Speak to them, look around to decipher the general age-group, ascertain if your cultural references are relevant and quickly assess their careers and stages of life. However, if you're speaking to board of directors of a large organization or several organizations, you may not have the luxury of mingling casually before you present. In that situation, you may want to do a quick background research of these specific individuals and their respective company profiles. If you're unable to do both, you can easily ask the organizer for the expected or targeted audience profile and work from there.

Here's why you should go through all this trouble and why it'll be worth it. By being aware of the characteristics and demographics of the people you speak to, you will be able to effectively tailor your presentation and pick your supporting points, anecdotes or analogies in order to reiterate what you need to say. Speaking to a group of 15-year-old students, for example, is very different from speaking to a group of 19-year-old students... much less an audience of professionals.

You'll find that audience-surveying is especially important when you're doing a technical presentation. In situations like that, you'll find that you need to assess your audience's level of awareness before you even craft your presentation so as to not bore or overwhelm them. Great public speakers understand that mistakes can always be overcome with connection, and information are greater shared with connection. If your audience is connected to you,

you're less worried about forgetting a point, making an awkward statement or even looking slightly disheveled. You're less anxious about what ifs such as "what if I fall?" "what if the projector breaks down and my slides are gone forever?" or "what if I pass gas on stage?" With a connection, you're automatically less worried as all will be forgiven.

#2 The all important Q&A session

- Remember to *not* point with your finger

- Maintain eye contact

- Do not sidetrack question; answer directly. If unsure, admit it or save for a backstage meeting

The all important Q&A session

It's not farfetched to say that most presenters are extremely relieved and extremely worried at the same time when they reach this stage of their speech. They're relieved that most of the talking is now over, but they are also deeply anxious about the type of questions that will come flying their way. If you find yourself in this position, remember to keep your cool and remember that the session is *still* within your control.

The general rule of thumb for dealing with questions is to listen to the question, answer it, and then quickly bridge it to your agenda. If you need a minute to think and gather yourself and the answer to your question, repeat the question for the rest of the audience. This also helps the rest of the audience be aware of what exactly you're addressing.

Firstly, when selecting which member of the audience's question to answer, remember to *not* point at them with your finger. In many cultures, this gesture is perceived as rude and aggressive. Instead, gesture at them with your palm faced upward, as if welcoming someone.

While answering the question, remember to maintain eye contact with the person who asked the question. If you can, give him/her a concise response and then move on to the next question. Maintain your credibility by offering facts to support your answer and always be diplomatic. If you're asked a question that's unrelated to your topic or completely outside of your field of expertise, you can politely explain the reason to why you're choosing to not answer that question or even covering the topic in your subject. If you find yourself faced with a question asked in an aggressive or particularly argumentative tone, my suggestion is to answer it briefly and quickly, and then immediately move on. Some questioners may try and trap you into a debate which is usually time-consuming and will bore the rest of the audience. Try your very best to avoid falling into an open debate with that individual by rephrasing their question and quickly moving on to the next.

There will also come a time when you find yourself unsure of the answer to someone's question. Truthfully, I believe in being honest and telling him/her that you really aren't sure if the answer you offer may be accurate. However, you can take it an extra mile by promising to gather information about the answer to be sure and get back to them. It's important, then, obtain that person's contact information from the organizer or the person himself and actually provide him with an answer, or at least an acknowledgment. Alternatively, you can offer the question to other members of the audience and see how they respond. In some situations, you may find yourself greeted with silence the moment you open up the Q&A session. Many speakers immediately move to close the session altogether and exit the stage. I personally think that if you're greeted with silence, you've either (a) lost the audience completely, or (b) got a really shy audience. If you've done everything by the book and how I've advised you to, the latter option is the most definitely the correct answer. If you're speaking to a primarily Asian audience, you're less likely to be bombarded by questions. In that situation, I would suggest *not* closing the session and instead share the answers to some frequently asked questions about your presentation topic. This way you're covering all bases and making sure that you deliver added value to your audience now that the presentation is over.

#3 Getting your audience engaged

- Icebreaker at the start of session

- If group is large, split audience into smaller groups for short activities

- Throw out an open question at the beginning of presentation

Getting your audience engaged

One of the keys to a truly successful presentation is audience participation. By involving your audience in the presentation, you're helping them focus and better-relate to the material you need to present, therefore encouraging them to take immediate action with the ideas you shared after the session. If you're wondering why you need to go the extra mile to get your audience to participate and actually *remember* and apply what you say, let me give you the answer. Your role as a speaker is not just to convey a message, but to also facilitate the absorption and the application of this message. A truly successful speaker truly cares for the audience.

One of the fastest and simplest ways to stimulate audience participation is in the form of an ice-breaker at the very start of the session. Ice-breakers are particularly useful for long seminars, but can also be used in shorter presentations to allow your audience to move around and shake things up before you actually begin. A good ice breaker is to start with asking all members of your audience to stand up and introduce themselves to at least 2 people around them and offer a short, quirky, random fact about themselves.

If you've got time and a large group, you can split your audience into small or partner groups and involve everyone in various activities. In order to fully maximize audience participation, you can even get these groups to elect a leader or a representative to share their findings and voice their unanimous thoughts.

During long sessions, it's easy for the audience to get either groggy or antsy. What you can do is to get them to start your session with warm-up exercises. Ask them to stand up, raise their arms up, and swing about, or even allow them to have a nice cat stretch. Another quirky way of getting them involved, interacting and awake is to get everyone to stand up and give the person next to them a 2-minute back rub. You can also get them up and moving by playing upbeat music and getting them in the groove for a quick shake and dance before you actually begin.

Another good way to actually connect with your audience and get them to interact with *you* is to throw out a question to them at the beginning of your presentation. A common but smart question is to ask them what they expect to gain from your session or speech and at the end of the session; you can review these points with members of your audience to show exactly what you've covered. This is a good way to allow your audience to connect the dots by themselves and actively search your presentation for key takeaways.

In some occasions, you may find yourself wishing to gather input from your audience. Let me share with you a simple and effective method to do so. This method is called the "Ben Franklin Close". The only materials you need are a whiteboard or flip chart and a marker. You start off by splitting the paper into two lengthwise and labeling each side of the paper - pros and cons for example. Then, you get your audience to shout out answers and ideas while you write them down. This not only stimulates their tired brains and gets them thinking, it also gives you a moment to quickly analyze your presentation, recoup, and decide on your next actions.

It's not unusual to be faced with awkward, less-sociable members of the audience. In more conservative cultures, open and casual communication and interaction is not the norm. In order to avoid awkward silences and stony glances, you can pre-select a handful of volunteers. This gives them time to prepare, and will fill an otherwise overly quiet session. In the situation where you have no response to your question, be prepared to actually answer it yourself. However, it's important to not take the silence too personally. Every public speaker has faced a stony or less sociable audience at a point in time.

One good way to encourage interaction is through "bribes". No, I'm not talking about the illegal kind. I'm referring to small "secret" gifts you can throw out to more bold and daring members of your audience to "reward" them for their participation. This can include inexpensive custom pens, notepads, folders or even key chains.

Last but not least, you have to remember that the goal of audience involvement and interaction is to inspire them to feel good about themselves and to motivate them to take action. Remember that people act for their own reasons, not yours. Therefore it's important to provide them with an environment within which they can act in response to your message.

Just a quick summary -- introduce ice-breakers into your session, suggest warm-up exercises or dance sessions to keep an upbeat and high flow of energy, get to know your audience and what they want to help them achieve their goals, offer small, inexpensive gifts to get them to participate and remember the goal of audience interaction.

#4 Items of preparation prior to your presentation

- Use cue cards

- Rehearse your opening and ending thoroughly and constantly

- Mind your uhms and ahs (aka 'brain farts')

- Monitor your audience

Items of preparation prior to your presentation

Now that you've covered the basics of speech preparation, speech personalization, vocal energy, body language and platform skills, audience surveying and audience engagement and interaction, you can move on to the final portions of this guide - the key items you need to get ready prior to your presentation. Here are a few quick tips to help make your presentation smooth-flowing.

First up, use cue cards. If you're unsure of your ability to memorize an entire speech, don't fret - no one really expects you to. With paper, you can easily create quick, point-formed cue cards to help you through an entire presentation. Many public speakers make the mistake of printing an *entire essay* on a bunch of cards. **Do not fall into that trap**. Remember the outline of your speech that you made at the very beginning of the speech-crafting process? Get that outline and flesh it out into a handful of cue cards.

Sprinkle short notes and reminders like "Tell funny pool story" or "Show chart about gender differences" throughout your cue cards instead of the full story itself. Cue cards are extremely useful elements in any presentation and like any other speaker out there; don't hesitate to employ the correct use of it.

Rehearse your opening and ending thoroughly and constantly. I said this before, and I will repeat it again because this is how important it is - Introduction is King. Remember that the first few minutes, or even *seconds*, of your speech determines the mood and flow of the rest of your presentation... and it even determines the amount of audience focus and attention.

Do not over-rehearse. Remember that it's really important to be **natural**. Rehearsing too much shows, and not in a good way either. While preparation *is* key, you also need to make sure that your presentation is conversational and natural, not memorized. Rehearse the full speech the night before your presentation, and then **stop**. Enough. Forget it.

Mind your uhms and ahs. That may sound silly, but in retrospect, it really isn't. You may not notice your ahs and uhms, but trust me -- your audience does. Watch what you say and keep them to a minimum.

Monitor your audience. The moment you sense that you're losing them and they're phasing out of the presentation, adjust your speech, improvise and project yourself forcefully. Alternatively, at this point of the presentation, you can quickly break and get them to get up and get moving with a quick warm up exercise before quickly repeating your initial points and moving on to the next one.

#4 Items of preparation prior to your presentation

• Get a good night's sleep the night before

• On the day of your presentation, **arrive early**

• Lastly, but most importantly, **have fun!**

Get a good night's sleep the night before. Why do I say that and why is it important? Because lack of sleep results in frayed nerves -- and that shows. When you're not sufficiently rested, you're more likely to succumb to nerves, hand jitters and stutters -- all of which damage not only your presentation, but your credibility. Avoid all that and if you're not a coffee-person, don't try to compensate for the lack of sleep with a cup of coffee. You'll find that caffeine does not *just* keep you awake, it keeps you over stimulated and less composed.

On the day of your presentation, **arrive early**. There are many benefits to arriving early. Firstly, you won't enter the venue like a wreck and waltz onto the stage unprepared. Arriving early allows you to run your points quickly in your mind prior to actually presenting. You'll also come across as cool, calm and collected - important components in conveying confidence. When you're not rushed, you're also less likely to forget things. Secondly, like I said before in this guide, arriving early allows you to mingle with your audience and get to know them better. Stand outside while they're registering and converse with them. Find out their hopes and dreams and know what they hope to gain from your session, or even why they attended at all. Simple things like that not only help **you** determine the tone of your presentation, but allow your audience to connect with you and get to know you. This way, you *know* that you already have friends in the audience and will be less likely to fear and be nervous.

Lastly, but most importantly, **have fun**. It may sound impossible, but there are neurons in your brain called "mirror neurons". Like their names, they mirror the actions of the person before you. If your energy is high and your tone upbeat, your audience will mirror the exact same thing. Vice versa if your energy is low and your tone monotonous - they will mirror boredom. You need to enjoy what you're talking about, and inject passion and enthusiasm into your presentation. In other words... you need to have fun.

9. Five Steps To Creating Incredibly Powerful Stories

Now that you have the basics of creating a stunning presentation, let's move on to another area that will help you increase your effectiveness even more. This last bit of information will take you over the edge. Have you ever wondered why some speakers are so much more fun to listen to even when you know they are trying to sell you something? It is the stories.

In the beginning of this book, we talked about the different benefits of stories. The goal of this chapter is to give you the added elements you need to create incredible and effective stories that will be remembered by your audiences for years to come. Some stories I have told are as far from the truth as can be…but there are friends of mine who still remember those stories and tell me how those stories have changed their lives.

I sometimes tell a made-up story about an old man I knew named Mr. Long. The story deals with the wisdom that Mr. Long shared with me before he dies. The purpose of the story changes from time to time depending on my message. One evening, after giving a speech using this story, a woman came to me with tears in her eyes. She began telling me how Mr. Long reminded her of her mother, who had passed away a year before. She was able to remember her mother, smile and receive the importance of the message…all from a man I created out of thin air. The benefits of storytelling in your presentation are enormous.

So how do we do it? How do we take our storytelling skills and go to the next level? Here are some basic guidelines for making your stories more memorable.

Step one: Tense.

No, I don't mean for you to get tense, I mean put your story in the present tense. We should always put as much of our story in the present tense as possible. Keep the action and the story fresh and unpredictable.

If you have a story where you experienced a near death situation, if you tell it in the past tense, your audience will get bored. Why? Your audience already knows the ending. They know you didn't die because you are standing there talking to them. However, if you put the same story in present tense, they will be so busy living the story with you that they will not even give thought to whether you died or not…the audience will be content to let you finish the story and wait on you to guide them through to the end of the story and to the point of your message.

When we listen to stories, we use our imagination to transport us into the story as an innocent on-looker. We love to imagine ourselves in the same situation and figure out what we would say, what we would do or what we would not do. That is why we like movies. The beauty of storytelling is that there are no limits on the person who paints a picture with words and there are no limits on what the audience can visualize during your story. Some of my favorite books are the ones that don't tell me every single detail about how a person looks, but gives me enough information to create my own mental picture of the characters in the story. Sometimes I visualized someone else, sometimes I visualized myself. With words, we can instantly connect with a group of people and take them all on a trip as one; and still allow each person an opportunity to individualize their experience with the story.

Always keep in mind that your listeners want to be involved in the story, so let them experience the story with you. Put the story in the present tense. Transport yourself to the exact moments the story took place. Report what you see- not what you saw. Report what you hear, not what you heard. Report what you do -not what you did. Take the journey again and let your audience come with you. Let your audience ride along, and they will feel full when you were finished.

Step number two: Creating Dynamic Characters

No matter what type of story you are enjoying (spoken, written or visual), it must have dynamic characters.

A story is always enhanced if you use at least one character other than yourself (the storyteller). The interactions between the characters in your story will be interesting because your characters are distinctly different individuals (unless you are going for the Stepford wives effect). The way you develop these distinctly different characters is by giving each character something special… something unique to them and to no one else in the story. As your storytelling abilities expand, you will become better at creating distinctions that will separate your character's personalities.

Why go through all this trouble? Why not just give the guys in the story deep voices and put your hands on your hips for the women? You don't do that because that is cheating your audience. There are over six billion people on earth, and each and every one of us has a desire to be recognized as an individual. Show your audience that your characters are real people with real personalities…just like them

So how does one make their characters more dynamic? We begin by using step one (tense). When we put our story in the present tense, we create opportunities for characters to enter into the story. No longer will our story be confined to just the storyteller. Putting our story in the present tense give us the opportunity to create at least one individual character in the story besides the storyteller.

Once we have a character in our story, we give each individual a distinct personality and a few individual "quirks" to make them more realistic. Perhaps you have a story with an elderly woman in it. Perhaps your elderly woman character walks with a limp and grinds her teeth when she talks. Maybe your uncle character has an eye patch, no front teeth and repeats his sentences a lot. Perhaps someone constantly blinks their eyes and fidgets constantly with their fingers. When you establish your characters, make them three dimensional by giving them "quirks" that only they have. This way, as you tell the story, each character lives on their own and the audience will be captivated.

It is important not to create too many characters for your stories, because it could begin to confuse your audience. Managing one or two characters In a story is quite enough, because you want the audience to get to know these characters so they will be invested in these characters.

With dynamic character creation, one of the main ideas to remember is that you want these characters to be distinct individuals. If you were telling a story about your Uncle John who is a heavy smoker and you told the story from Uncle John's perspective I might put in a smoker's cough or have Uncle John constantly do the motions of taking a drag from his cigarette…a simple gesture with a tremendous effect.

Don't Forget To Add The Drama!

Drama in a story usually comes to light through conflict…and we love it! Oh, I know most of us say we don't like drama. We say we don't want drama in our lives. Sometimes my wife walks through the house singing a song called "No More Drama" by Mary J Blige. But the truth of the matter is we love drama. We crave drama, whether it is packaged as a verbal story, a written story or a video based story. No matter what type of story you are telling, there is a drama or at least opportunity for drama. Why? Because our stories usually involve people; opposing wills. There is even opportunity for struggle, with just one character. Who is not familiar with personal struggle?

In order to create drama in a story, let's use what I call the "Uh Oh, Oh My God" technique.

*All five of the steps you are learning can be used on stories you have already created, or they can be used to create an original story. If you were creating an original story, then step 3 May be the step you want to start with.

Uh Oh, Oh My God

Let's talk about the stories you already love. It could be a written story, a visual story, or a verbal story. Most of the stories you love have the following technique imbedded in them. I call it the Uh Oh, Oh my God technique.

Here is how it works;

We meet the main characters of a story. We get to know the character by seeing them interact with other characters, listening to their point of view, watching them move forward with their lives. Then all of a sudden there is an **Uh Oh**- a problem occurs that could throw everything off track. Perhaps Young love is tested by an "ex" coming into the picture. Maybe the perfect person for the mission rejects the mission. Perhaps Sunday dinner is interrupted by alien space ships entering the atmosphere.

Whatever the scenario, there is the introduction of the first "Uh Oh", the first hiccup in an otherwise smooth storyline. The "Uh Oh" gives your story a "next level", a problem to overcome.

Now that our story has some additional depth, it seems more like the life we know. If adding a first "uh oh" moment does not satisfy your goals in the story, don't be afraid to add another "uh oh" moment. You can have more than one. As soon as one thing goes wrong, something else seems to goes wrong. Has that happened to you? Have you ever stopped in the middle of a situation and said, "what else can possibly go wrong"? Yes? Then you are now ready for an "Oh My God" moment.

Oh My God Moment

The introduction of an "oh my god" moment is crucial.

This is where the story takes an unexpected turn for the absolute worse. This is where the conflict in the story is so enormous that it threatens to destroy all of the progress the characters have made.

In the most engaging of stories, the "oh my god" moment gives your character an incredible hurdle to overcome, thereby proving your message in the story. Once an "oh my god" moment has been reached, we can close out the story by having the characters overcome this final huge obstacle.

Step four; truth

"… It doesn't have to be a true statement; it just needs to be stated truly".

-Elliott Eddie

All good stories have a line of truth that forms the basis of that story, just like most good jokes. I'm not saying that every story must be true, just that there must be elements in the story that ring true to your listeners.

For example, if I were to tell you a story about a five year old child who was hit by a car and his 5 foot two inch mother lifted the car off the child's to get him free, would you believe me? Perhaps you would. Why?

Perhaps you would believe me because we know that when our adrenaline is flowing and there is an immediate threat, it is possible to display more strength than you are normally capable of displaying. So the above story would be a believable story. If I were talking with someone and trying to convey the message that when the moment of truth comes, you will have the strength to do what you need to do, I could use this story as an example because it proves my point.

However, if I told you that same story and said that the mother lifted the car off her child and then threw the car over her shoulder, you would probably no longer believe me. Why? Because I have destroyed the truth of my story. In telling this story I make an agreement with my audience. I agree to lead them on a plausible pathway to realize a message that will better their lives and they agree to listen to my story and take my message to heart- as long as I remain true to them.

However, when I introduce information that is not plausible within the story or stretches the truth beyond the limits of the world I have created, my audience no longer trusts me. I have lost them in that moment. Even if I have the greatest message in the world, once I lose my audience's trust it does not matter; they're not listening to me anymore with an open heart to consider my point.

It is entirely possible to give your audience a story that says the mother picks the car off the child and tosses the car over her shoulders, if you make an agreement with your audience from the beginning that allows you to do that. What I mean is, if you present your story in a way that everyone knows it is fiction or that portions may be an embellishment, the audience will gladly follow you to the Moon and back. That means you can create whatever you want and they will accept it because they accepted the beginning premise.

For the most part, truth is a check that we will put our stories through to make sure that it is related to our targeted audience. The questions you can ask yourself that pertains to truth are;

Do the characters react in a way that is true on a human level? Do the characters display an emotion or mindset that my audience can relate to? Is the conflict the characters face one that everyday people can understand? (This is not an exhaustive list of questions).

What if the premise is fiction? As long as the characters you give in the story react to the various situations true to the emotions that your audience is familiar with, your audience will go along with your fictional story.

When you hear someone say the story was farfetched or it just wasn't believable, what they are saying to you is that the characters did not connect with them on a basic human level.

Step five; Humor

Let's chat a bit about humor in your story. With the guidelines in this book, your stories will be full of heart; and heart always wins over humor. However, you will still want to include humor in your story.

Humor can help in a number of ways. Humor will give your audience a break during the message to gather themselves and not become overwhelmed with information. Humor can make uncomfortable information a little more palatable. Humor will draw in an audience and help them relax a bit so they can understand your message. Humor does a lot to help make your presentation more dynamic. But how do you include humor? What if you are not a funny person? How do you *"do"* humor?

There are tons of books with valuable information on the steps you can take to create humor. Yes there are techniques like the rule of three and so on. However, I want to give you a simpler way to create natural humor in your speeches and presentation.

I believe that the best humor in a presentation is humor that is honest to the human condition. From our young reading careers and from life itself, we may remember that comedy is born from tragedy. The stories that make us smile and laugh now are often the same ones that made us cry or caused us pain.

Hearing someone react to a situation that we have faced ourselves will often produce its own humor. Expressing what we were thinking at the time of conflict is a great way for humor to come out on its own.

There are different ways to achieve humor.

Humor can be born from re-enactments. If you are having a conversation with the 10 year-old child in your story, use your dynamic characters tutorial to bring out the personalities of the 10 year-old child. The interaction between the child and yourself will often create its own humor.

Use facial expressions and body language to express what your characters are thinking and experiencing. Your audience wants to be included- they want to connect to the story. Don't push them, just allow them a chance to see a fully rounded character and they will create their own moments for laughter...and they will love you for it.

Other opportunities for humor inside a story include exaggerate the actions or mannerism of characters. Make it big.

Acting out the events of your story. If one of your characters is a dancer, give the audience a few moves when you introduce the character. It is even better if you are not a dancer. The audience will appreciate you trying to show them something that you are not good at. It shows you are human, which make them feel better about their own shortcomings.

Experiment with the speed of your story. Perhaps a portion of the action happens in slow motion and you share it in slow motion. This is a bit more physical, but if you reach for it, the audience will come with you and hold you up.

Use references to memories that your audience is familiar with. Perhaps a character in your story gets hit in the head and develops a Flintstone size knot. People who remember the cartoon "The Flintstones" and have not seen it in decades will remember it and at least smile if not laugh. Your audience will be involved in the story. When the story is over and it supports your overall message, they will feel like you took them on a journey in which they picked up a gem that will help improve their lives in some way.

Humor may seem like a hard thing to put in speeches because we're often working too hard to make it fit. Humor is shared when one person tells a story with elements that another person is familiar with, even if they have not gone through the exact same thing. I have heard women tell stories about childbirth and the interesting situations they have faced. I have not personally been through childbirth, but I can laugh because I understand the truth that underlines the story. I can understand pushing through pain. I can understand things going wrong around you at a critical moment. That is why I laugh at those stories, because in some way or another, I can relate.

You don't have to change your storytelling style. You don't have to try to become a person you are not when you give a presentation. All you really want to do is use some basic techniques to take your storytelling abilities to the next level. You want to understand what it is that your audience wants from you while you're on stage, so you can do a better job in giving them what they need. In return they will follow you on the journey to uncover your message.

 A gentleman named Bill Grove once said,

"Tell a story make a point".

I say,

"Tell a better story and secure your future".

Learning to tell better stories will help you secure that investment or loan. Telling a better story will increase your opportunities. Telling a great story might even get you out of a speeding ticket.

Whether your goal is to teach a lesson or put yourself in an upwardly mobile position, telling better stories is the key you need to increase your lot in life. And it will make your stories a lot more fun to listen to.

About the Author

Elliott Eddie is an awarded, worldwide distributed Actor, writer, director, filmmaker, editor and Author. Elliott started his professional entertainment career as a production assistant on "B.E.T's ComicView in 1998 and was promoted to "segment producer" in the same season. Elliott went on to be instrumental in the show's highest television rating season through creativity and attention to details.

As an actor, Elliott has been in films distributed worldwide such as 'Galactic Raiders', 'Coast' and 'Issues' among other films. As a producer/filmmaker, Elliott Eddie has produced movies that are distributed around the world –including through Amazon OnDemand, Blockbusters and Netflix. Movie Titles include; The Wisdom of Solomon, Apocalypse Rising, The Memoirs of Frank White, Unborn Sins and Peepholes Vol: I-IV. Mr. Eddie's first film, "Unborn Sins" has had over 12 million downloads and appears in 13 languages.

In addition, Mr. Eddie is an experienced entrepreneur. Currently the CEO & Chairman of DM Media Incorporated, Elliott has grown a business that is successful in several areas. From Tax Preparation to Defensive Driving Schools…from film/television/book distribution to real estate investment, Mr. Eddie has a plethora of information to share with those looking to improve their situation and status in life.

LIMITS OF LIABILITY / DISCLAIMER OF WARRANTY:

The Author has strived to be as accurate and complete as possible in the creation of this manual and does not warrant or represent at any time that the contents within are the latest trends due to the rapidly changing nature of the Internet.

The Author assumes no responsibility for errors, omissions, or contrary interpretation of the subject matter herein. Any perceived slights of specific persons, peoples, or organizations are unintentional.

This book is not intended for use as a source of legal, business, accounting or financial advice. All readers are advised to seek services of competent professionals in legal, business, accounting, and finance field.

Any screen shots seen in this manual are from publicly accessible files and web pages and used as "fair use" for reporting purposes and to illustrate various points mentioned herein. Texts and images available over the Internet may be subject to copyright and other intellectual rights owned by third parties.

www.ingramcontent.com/pod-product-compliance
Lightning Source LLC
Chambersburg PA
CBHW072211090426
42740CB00012B/2479